We Are The Weather
Jim McElroy

smith|doorstop

the poetry business

Published 2022 by
Smith|Doorstop Books
The Poetry Business
Campo House,
54 Campo Lane,
Sheffield S1 2EG

Copyright © Jim McElroy 2022
All Rights Reserved

ISBN 978-1-914914-06-5
eBook ISBN 978-1-914914-07-2
Typeset by The Poetry Business
Printed by People for Print, Sheffield

Smith|Doorstop Books are a member of Inpress:
www.inpressbooks.co.uk

Distributed by NBN International, 1 Deltic Avenue,
Rooksley, Milton Keynes MK13 8LD

The Poetry Business gratefully acknowledges
the support of Arts Council England.

Contents

7	Hoor
9	The Oak Tree
10	Doodlebugs
11	Bully
12	Sacrificed
13	Coal Hole
14	The Attic Room
15	Hard Knocks
16	Spray Gun
17	Sheep Carcass
18	Pouring the Yard
19	Weatherbeaten
20	The Auctioneer is Selling Our Cow
22	Enough
23	Noirish
24	Audit at the Slaughter House
25	His Work
26	Everything Related
28	The Crows
29	Shit Happens
31	My Father's Store
32	Unmaking His Chair
34	Second Chances
35	A Message from The Dead

i.m. Bernard McElroy 1927–1990

Hoor

He called Widow Welsh *that poor oul hoor*,
in winter he'd send me up with fresh eggs;
next door, Joe McNab was *tight oul hoor*,
said he would count every bleedin' penny;
the *right oul hoors* lived on the Rock Hill,
I was let play with their *right wee hoors*.
Passing pedlars, scammers, were all *cute hoors*,
the tax man, a *connivin little hoor's bollix*.

I followed his hobnail crunch, oily overalls,
round the farm, *annoyin his hoorin head*:
too many questions, *go ask your mother*.
At school, if I passed exams, he gave me
right quick wee hoor. Out on the moor,
neck veins bulging like baler twine,
he'd scrum hug boulders into position,
build ditches; at stubborn stones, sleeve
off brow sweat, stare at its granite belly,
christen it *a heavy oul hoor*; over lunch,
on top of stones, he'd share out soda farls,
cheddar slabs, pour our *cuppa tay*, tell me
thank your Mother; as he lit his pipe,
he'd point out hedges needing trimmed,
the opening crops: ripening corn, barley.

When I left for the city, autumn's thresher
was gulping sheaves of wheat; I watched him
grimace as he kneed obese seed bags up
to the trailer; through the belt slew, baler hum,
he yelled *mind yourself*, to watch out for all
them cute hoors. Later that winter, the switch

put her call through, told me, *your mother's
on the line* – I was to *come home quick.*

Still in his overalls, he lay on the bed; fresh
muck clung to his hobnails: *right oul hoor*
found him slumped over granite; I bent down
for our first kiss – his *hoorin head*, cold as stone.

The Oak Tree

In the field, we climbed into the oak bough.
The eldest took the bow-saw to its crown.
Branches splintered off, whished to earth,
became farm machinery that we attached
to the drawbars of our arms. Our lips
spluttering tractor noises, we raced past
the barn gable and their leafy canopies
bounded behind us. We threshed, reaped,
ploughed, trampled paths across pastures.

At tight spots age held sway: the youngest
pulled in for trailed widths of combine, binder,
baler, wagged through the passing imagined.
Queued for refuelling, we were Slurry Bill,
Harvester Bell, Backaway Barley, Cart Knox.
On the road home, we'd race up The Scallion,
freewheel at Winnie's, drop a gear on Dandy's,
pootle over crossroads, toot toot hellos, cheerios.

Even the smallest twigs were of use; pared struts
made gun butts, rifles; hard forks were catapults
with which we slayed Goliaths. Under cover
of its crown, our penknives carved the year
and our initials into the trunk. In the parch
of autumn the bare sticks were harrow-pin,
grubber teeth. Dragging the dying behind us,
our play rustled back and forth past its bark.
Kicking up its cast-offs, we reaped, sowed,
and compressed the seasons while on the trunk
the oak's regrowth pushed out the nicked years.

Doodlebugs

Behind the barn where thistles, nettles,
grew through old cartwheels, axles,
the flat hearts of doodlebugs pulsed
under what had been discarded.
The mute frequencies of their low lives
unheard under the clang and clatter
of farm work, the chunter of tractor engine.

Hiding where the risk of drying out
was low, the gill pads of their feet
rummaged the brown bin of earth, sought
the damp lands of crustacean ancestors.

After dark, safe from beak of hen, duck,
the looming shadows of hob and hoof,
their uropods fanning from compost,
they put out feelers and scuttled out.

In summer days, lift slates, planks, off
their hidey holes and the dark was gone.
Homeless amidst bramble, marram, rye,
they hid their young in the brood pouches
of their underbellies, the moulting plates
of their grey backs ran round in circles:
the daylight blazed into their underworld.

Bully

The bullfrog hopped onto the bog stone.
Killen's fingers, thick
as a bullock's tongue, grabbed it.

Stabbing corn straw into its arse,
he pursed his slobbering lips;
eyes narrowing, his cheeks crimson
as slapped buttocks,

he filled his lungs and blew.
I watched the throat tighten,
its pupils growing into black discs,
until, veins dilated and strung like a drum,

the bullfrog burst.
Amongst the splattered docken,
its blood clots hung like fuchsia.

Sacrificed

Her mother died at the birth, I was surrogate.
Daily, I rattled the yard gate,
watched her full fleece
spring and buck towards me.

For months, clamped like a magnet,
the bottle shot volts up my arms,
her urgent gulps nudging my midriff,
the milk line lowering like a syringe.

Unannounced, a reversing lorry
darkened the yard; tailgate clattering concrete.
The lorryman strode over, grabbed her neck.
I stared as she scuttled up the ramp.

The gangplank slammed shut,
drowned her bleats, flared nostrils
nosed through air holes.
The lorry shuddered into the dusk.

Coal Hole

Dad's sent me out for coal. The full moon
shines like a miner's light. In the link shed,
crows doze on the steel cross beams,
hens roost in coops. At the barn gable,
the downspout drips to a full barrel,
implements cast shadows of the gone day.

I tiptoe through the yard's dark stare
to the grey breeze-block of the bunker,
eye its gape and hear his warning:
watch out for the bogeyman. Inside,
cornered coals scowl, their wet rubble
bleeds a black blood. In the Dandy,
Desperate Dan lifts a cow in one hand,
his stubble's so thick it needs a blowtorch.
I stick my chin out, reach in, my shovel
scrapes screed, hoarse coal grumbles,
rumbles on, scores my scuttle's enamel.
I lug their coarse jowls across the yard
to the house door. The scullery latch rattles.

Back in the living room, we sit at the fire.
Did you see him? I shake my head.
He leans in and strikes a Bo-Peep:
kindling flickers, anthracite sparks,
and belches light, flames rage up the flue.
The chimney growls, a down draught
billows from the hearth, bobs on the breast.
The night's clock ticks time on the mantle.

The Attic Room

The skylight holds a harvest moon, spills light
on my brothers' sleep. Topped and tailed,
I'm in the middle, their feet at my nose.
I've been awake for hours thinking about
what Michael said, and as his tugged blanket
yawns and falls, the drawn warmth
of the gable breast thaws the chill,
I know that under the slated eaves
pinched eyes are squinting at the ridge,
claws grip on rafter, prep for the ascent.

Then, the humped sprint: the night's mice
skitter up the angle, skip past lath, purlin,
race the hard yards to the heat. Below
the peak, claws thresh, loosen a scree;
plaster scatters and mice slew down the angle
to the wall plate. I squirm under the blanket,
and beneath the bed I hear them darting past
the full po, nibbling at satchels, shoe laces,
comics, taking the bait: the set trap snaps,
my younger brother's urine soaks my spine.

Hard Knocks

Hind legs splayed like pylons, hooves
anchor her. Blind with birthing, she pushes
the calf head out, the neck flops above the four foot drop.

Like blackthorn sticks, forelegs slither through;
haunches test her taut vulva; spine arched as a bridge,
cramped innards retch her burden home. The greased head

plummets, thumps stone; birth heat splashes
the cold byre. Like switched electric, dark eyes brighten,
her calf shudders, hoofs through mucus. Thrashing sparse straw,

trumpet nostrils gulp air; sprockling up,
the shadows jerk life into mortar and forelegs splay,
the hocks steady the stagger: hooves set ready for the hard knocks.

Spray Gun

Up to his knees in leaf, potato sprayer strapped on his back, Uncle Dan towers over the stalks. He strides the hill, his left hand pumps a lever, the nozzle in his right showers a bleach-blue spray that drums the leaf.

He marches up. The sloshing sprayer gives off a gas that stings my tongue. He winks, gives the thumbs up and rustles past, lush stalks brushing his overalls, his shins soaked blue. I leave for school, my satchel a sprayer, like Uncle Dan's.

Home from school, the field lies bare. Bald drills line the hill like brown corduroy, dead leaves limp in the furrow, parched stalks thinned to wisps of greying hair.

I stare at his bedspread: Uncle Dan lies still, his closed eyelids are sunk in his skull. A wake-wind whispers how he went down quick, how it ate holes in him.

In my dreams, bleached teeth nibble flesh, his razed skeleton rises off the bed, death-blue skin ripped to shreds, holed shinbones hollow as a flute.

>   Ill winds whistle in
>   blue blood bowls in deep footprints
>   we close the windows

Sheep Carcass

Picked rib hoops, bone knuckle juts
at rump, hock, flank; the seized forelegs
stiff as whinroot: a landed sparrowhawk
flaps on the scapula, gold irises hold me
in its field. I keep my distance, watch
the claws knead, beakhook jerk at gaunt elastic
of sinew, cartilage. A chawn ear tag at my feet.

The skull's wedge is stripped of its wimple,
her once blackface gone. The jaw's clench
has the look of a grin. On the fetlock,
a winged fist of blowflies. Below, I spot
the crusted, swollen cloven that held her back.

The midges hum a halo, blue-green shimmers
of blowflies buzz over the night's raw feast.
Nothing wasted of her bloat, this abandoned hill
now holds high her bones: her gone udder
that will never suckle, that no birth lamb will nuzzle.

This leaving sparrowhawk flap-flap glides
across the fenceline, where wool of the gone flock
twists on the barbs. I follow the flight path:
blunt tail, wingspan, undulating to its high soar.
I think of built nests, gaping beaks, fledging life.

Pouring the Yard

We shovel sand and stones into the chunter,
shake in cement. The gravel scratch
of crushed aggregate scrapes
in the mixer's churn; hosed-in water
dampens the crackle of the mortar's
lime reaction. The steel belly tilts
to the turn of the dump wheel,
remade earth slithers from its iron pout,
slumps on the ground, buries
hoof pock, boot print, rut of cartwheel.

The concrete's moist slurp greying our boots,
our shovels shunt its mass across
the sections, spread its clad to the party wall
of the link shed; tamper planks
race the hardening time, slap it flat,
agitate in ridges, angle gullies for run-off.

The poured yard drying, hosed-on gallons
slake its drouth, seep to the darkness beneath.
Bunkered earth gulps its pallid leech;
bugs, slaters, scuttle for cover, worms, grubs,
squirm deep, root growth diverts for light.
Concrete ripples stiffen across the screed,
its load bearing ridges grip for tyres.

Weatherbeaten

My Father took the weather personally,
watched buds unfurl in whispers,
the low sun fix its eye on sticky petals.
The skies spring cleaned, let him work
in quick skifts. The clouds swept out rains,
watched his retreats to the shed.
Its tinny discussions beat the roof,
spouts gushed to gable barrels, overflowed
to Buchan traps. Downpours made a river
of the Hill Road. On Radio 4,
Athlone, he listened for forecasts, saw
the mercury drop on the hall barometer.

The wet patter eased, wider isobars of highs
circled in the pulsed ripple of puddles.
The sun cast its width, swole blisters
on road tar; bullocks snogged the lusty grass.
On the breeze, the pollen whoosh of rye,
and *boysadear*, the hay fever sneeze.
Then the mood swing: June's parched glare
lowered the reservoir, caked earth
cried out for water; tightening isobars
swooped, winds swirled, reeled him in.
His eyes would peel the horizon
as the wielded knives of Siberian easts
hacked his cheeks, ripped off petal and leaf.
In the verge, grounded leaves buried each other.

The Auctioneer is Selling Our Cow

His gavel knock knocks, bidding arms lean on the guard rail,
the handler hawthorns her round, and she's—*at three,
at three, three ten, thank you sir, fifteen, thirty,
at three thirty, now forty, who'll give me forty.*
She's spent her head-down life behind hedges,
ate round yellow petal of buttercup, white garland of oxeye,
and—*at three thirty, ten, forty*—a hawthorn's poking
the blonde whorl of her flank past the amped blah
of—*three fifty, sixty, eighty, lovely Charolais, and at four,
four ten, fifteen, thirty, forty*—the following eyes
size up her hind, her side eyes know the hard grazing,
green stain—*fifty*—of the mart screed's not the bent grass
of Keenan's meadow, the ring's fluorescent glare's not
the morning's haze over Croob, and as cap tip,
brow scratch, index flick lifts it to—*four sixty, and ten,
and ten, four eighty, on the market, five, and at five*—
the dark histories of her eyes say all she's ever done
is give her daily buckets of milk, suckled yearlings,
and his practised stammer says—*fifteen, and forty, and five,
forty five, five fifty*—and—*fifty five*—echoes over

the bullock roars, jump rails of outside lots and—*at five sixty,
and five, at sixty five*—her tail lifts, at—*seventy, and ten,*
her pats splatter the screed, steam on his—*five eighty,
six, and ten, at six ten, now twenty*—and his hyped chant
—*thirty, bid me ten, at six thirty, and five, and five, six forty,
at six forty*—the hawthorn slaps the blonde sweat
of her cheek, turns her round and—*at six fifty*—the dark misery
of her eyes stare in the mart must, sees no oats, no drinkers,
and—*at six fifty, ten, six sixty*—the muzzle-dark

of her nostrils froth on her stopped cud and—*seven, at seven*—
she needs to quench her drouth at Keenan's brook—
at seven ten, seven ten—nuzzle her nose in barley oats,
and their headshakes say no, slow his seven-ten prattle,
and—*at seven ten, seven ten, don't miss her, twenty,
and selling, at twenty, seven twenty*—bidding arms fold
on the guard rail—*at seven twenty, last call, last call*—
the black histories of her eyes see no feeding trough
by the steel fencing, welds, of the holding pen—*and at
seven twenty, last call, and selling*—her handler hawthorns
her round, the gold rivers of her urine run the ribbed incline
of the exit ramp, and at the—*and Sold*—his gavel knocks her down.

Enough

My sweaty belly button is full of seed hay:
no more will I stook sheaves in threes,
stand these hay teepees in their own reaped sward.
I won't sned turnips, my soaked knees roped
in the mealy jute of Sow and Weaner bags.
My stooped days are gone. Your stubbled harvest
can bristle; I won't bend to the sod,
or gather Arran Banners, fill baskets, bag for trailers.
No longer will I stand by turnip cutters,
my bored arm numbed in its turnings,
their sliced heads filling buckets for sows, store pigs.
No more shall our cow slap her shitty tail
across my cheek as I bend to the milking;
keep your dirt, your gutter muck. No more
shall I shovel dung through groop holes
of byre walls, watch it steam on the caked pats.
Farewell farm, stable, barn: this world can feed itself.

Noirish

The rising jumbo tipped a wing to the small fields
of Ireland and the shamrock nose

of Aer Lingus rose through clouds, banked for the land
of the free, then dipped through time zones

to the heat blast of Idlewild and you in your wool suit sweating
on the Saint Christophers she'd stitched

in the lapel with your licence getting you a start to your days
delivering NBC reels

through the honk and the blare of Manhattan, Queens,
Staten Island, The Bronx,

and your drive turning you to study and night school
and your sweet talking getting you

in the door, the lift humming you up to your Emmy Awards
and your Cadillac taking

the freeway to the maple streets of the New Jersey suburbs,
the tyres crunching

the gravel by the FOR SALE sign of your first house hunt
and the realtor showing you in

to your view from the bay window of the sign staked in the lawn:
NO BLACKS, NO DOGS, NO IRISH.

Audit at the Slaughter House

Out in the stockyard, bolt guns poof, bullock eyes jolt,
shatter like clays.

In the plant, the stock hangs in lines that echo my pinstripe:
strained muscles stretch like steeplechasers,
shin shavings pile as chaff.

Production starts: carcasses wallop on winches,
reel past hind pullers, rattle across the plant
to the process lines, stop. Skinned rumps jostle, slap.

In hair nets, white jackets flecked with blood,
gangers check batches, stamp rumps,
number the hinds in purple ink.

Down the line, process workers banter over organs,
sort the insides. I track my sample, note numbers,
follow to cold storage.

Forklifts whirr past, cart drums of hooves: offal trembles,
hums in barrels. In the cold store, shoulder
to shoulder, frozen herds hang like a stopped gallop.

At the rear, an open roller door; branded vans rev
on the weighbridge, screens flicker yields, weights.
As I note the hung tonnage, take stock,

my audit ticks flick like a bullock's tail.

His Work

was a clabbered boot rasping
on shovel-disrupted gravel.
The essential sweat
of the stooped day dripping
to penitential fields,
bent to the drill,
fingernails clotted in sod.

So when I returned home
in my pinstripe,
his spat tobacco hit the fire
like an exocet,
argued and sizzled
in the blushed turf of his work.

Everything Related

In the barn, straight-backed, the shovels
were brothers. Tallest, the long-tailed
gave leverage; washed at the gable tap,
its tapered mouth shone like a steel leaf.
The wide-mouthed navvy was for grip,
its ash shaft topped with a handle.
The workaholic spade was their rival.

The sharp tongues of sheep shears, scythe,
sickle. The steel glint of slashhook, hatchet,
his sharpening stone welting their lead edge.
His wagging index finger; shafts handed
to his *gimme*, the implements between us.
Tools had his features – tough nose
of pick and crowbar, the strong jaw
of claw hammer, jemmy. Grey eyes
of rivets that attached head and handle.

The many partners of the Massey: hook-ups
with buck-rake, binder, flatbed trailer.
Drawn loads of seed hay, barley bales,
gathered potatoes. On the road home,
pipe smoke wafting past his flat cap,
the tut-tutting of her diesel engine.
Down trenches, piping the eight inch
to the cattle drinkers. The ring of pick
on rock. Glacial whoof of broke stone.

At wet spells, knee on the loft's oil drum.
Sawn planks. The steel pant of hacksaw blade,
mizzle of filings. His glances out at the weather.
On Sundays, after first mass, tobacco smoke
rising over the copings, watching him talk
at the chapel wall. The Monday, half arc
of the final blow. The pick ringing as he fell.

The Crows

skip to the phone wires, close their claws
on the hum. Their military lines mimic

the night, stare at the skyline where sheep
fluff into hills, deep veins of trees

syphon slopes, drumlins go to ground.
The dark snoops around primrose,

jade, lavender; hedges bow
to the ditched fields, colours

rinse from clay, sink to their wells.
The purple dusk goes grey as the road.

The standing day laid down, cud churns
of the herd chaw into the dark,

in the yard, beak and bill turn in, Scruff
yawns into the night, paws the asleep day.

And then its inrush: loft steps
collapse into gables, roof lines drop,

phone wires reel in the distance, the poles
tumble to the pitch. It all falls black as the crows.

Shit Happens

Before the Rising, Gramps built the Low House.
Oul Boy told us that *turf blushed in the hearth*
as Gran nursed her three sons under the thatch.
Staring at the rotted door, I couldn't imagine them
living in there: all winter we'd knifed twine,
swished out bedding, put hay in the cattle's manger,
saw their cud churn, tartled hooves compact the chaw.

Our Pete pokes the dung, mutters *it's up to us now*.
I grab my graip, think how Gran'd turn in her grave
at the state of her kitchen. We fill the barrow,
I wheel it to the field; grass tufts on last year's pats:
I hear Oul Boy, *fork it out well*, he'd order,
that shite carpets the cattle's summer home.

We graip their mess, open a path, dung beetles
colonise the dungface, their slick husks black
as the bullocks' eyes. Under the hoof press,
they'd scavenged manure, cased their eggs in balls
of shit and sealed them in with their own spittle;
once born, they'll burrow out, he'd said. Our hands
blister on the shaft, the level lowers to the cobbles.
Pete says the baby beetles have it sorted: *never
go nowhere without their own home, even if they
lose it, all they need is nicked shit and their own spit.*

In the Rising, the thatch got torched; Oul Boy heard it.
His elder brothers scarpered, *sailed and signed
at Ellis Island*, he said. After that, Gramps built
the Hill House. Pete figured he felt safer higher up.

My graip prangs on the cobbles, I think of Gran
up there in her kitchen, sitting by the window,
praying, fingering beads, until the cholera got her.
I asked who burnt it: he cleared his throat, went silent.

It took us till lunch to dig them out; the cattle
lingered inside the door and their eyes kept looking.
Don't shoo them out, Oul Boy had told us,
their cud churn calls that grass up. We rested
on the ditch. I thought about homes, how they come
and go. Gran, Gramps, Oul Boy, all gone, uncles
laid in another continent my cousins call home,
how life churns on, just like the bullocks' cud.
That's how it is, Pete mused, *shit happens;
and anyway, they're pushin' up them daisies.*

The cattle clomped out and daylight spilled in.
Above the bricked-up hearth, Oul Boy's scythe
rusted in the rafters, spiders spun their webs,
the forked tails of barn swallows waggled
in the gable, flitted between muck puddle, eave,
mud nests domed on the purlins. The dung beetles
scuttled out, pittered past our barrow of shit, and
in the field, the bullocks' cud muttered the grass up.

My Father's Store

Hobnailed boots
crunching the gravelled laneway
fall silent crossing the wet summer sward
to the store.

The rusted latch no longer lifts
to swing open the doors, his veined hand
no longer flicks the switch
to lighten the dark,

gold grain rising
like a sand dune; no more the forward stoop,
no shovel scrapes the trowelled floor
to rise the billowed stour.

His old shovel's shine's dulled,
the white enamel bucket is open-mouthed,
sloped grain greying in its sunk centre
like hollowed cheekbone.

Even the dust has left the air.

Unmaking His Chair

        Wrought hands
          unweave the woven rope,
            to reveal the square seat frame.
   Wood stains unseep,
   and release the ash-sweet scent,
   until skin-pale wood
   stands bare.
         His mallet taps
          pop out each dowel pin,
          and unjoint the tenoned ends.
In loft light's chisel glint,
clinking dowels drop,
and each chip unchops,
         the auger bit uplifts,
         timber rinds uncurl,
         his drill unwhirrs.
             The sawing elbow stops,
             saw teeth withdraw,
             the pencil tip
             undraws the marking lines,
                    wood shavings
                    shimmer up,
                    the edgy skelfs relax.
               His bent back rises,
               curling grains regrip,
               brow sweat
               unbeads to pore –

          rings ripple out,
          the trunk rebuilds.

                    He stoops,
                    gnarled fingers grip,
                    his shoulder hoiks
                    the fresh cut trunk,
          the bark-wrapped ash
          points to its copse.

     His working boots
     crunch up the path,
     back to the wood,
          axe chips arc back,
          the ash reroots,
          and shook earth settles:
sap blood pumps,
closed arteries unfur,
the trunk heart beats.

Second Chances

My heart missed a beat.
They said it was the circuits,
a series of electrical impulses,
flashing around the veins, headlights in the dark.
Little nodules have grown in there like speed bumps.
When a beat hits one, it takes flight like a car, spins off.
So my heart goes bump, bump, bumpity, bump.
Instead of four, only three finish:
the beat that hits the bumpity,
flies off into the ether.

In coronary care,
my vein bumps ablated – the nurse
taking my pulse is telling me my lost beats are back,
and I'm suddenly at the night my Ford Anglia missed the hairpin,
took off through the hedge, shot past the big oak, pylons,
paling posts, barbed wire hanging off her underside,
headlights in flight like shooting stars,
four wheels thumping down
the right way up

amongst
the field of scattering sheep,
as the powers that be kept their chequered flag down,
my eighteen year old self awaking blind drunk in the ditch,
thanking my lucky stars the headlights
stayed lit.

A Message from The Dead

The night is lost to you.

Even in light
you don't see us.

We stir the air
bend branches, ripple waters

shake the ground,
blow your hair.

You think we are
the weather.

Acknowledgements

My gratitude to judges Daljit Nagra and Pascale Petit for selecting *We Are The Weather* for the International Book and Pamphlet Competition, to all at The Poetry Business and to my publishers, Smith|Doorstop, especially Ann and Peter Sansom. To my fellow poets, Dean Browne, Maya C Popa and Anastasia Taylor-Lind, it is a privilege to share this award with you.

Thank you to the editors of the following publications, in which versions of some poems have appeared: *Poetry Ireland Review, Gutter, Irish Times, The Rialto, New Humanist, Community Arts Partnership – Poetry in Motion Anthologies* (2018 and 2021), *Skylight 47*, Poetry Ireland Introductions ebook: *Incredible Things Do Happen* (2019), *Bridport Prize Anthology* (2019).

A selection of these poems have also been given recognition by award bodies: grateful acknowledgement is due to the 2021 Seamus Heaney New Writing Award, the 2020 Francis Ledwidge Award, the 2019 Poetry Ireland Introductions Award; for the 2020 Fingal Poetry Prize and 2019 Bridport Poetry Prize runner-up awards; and for shortlistings by the 2020 Rialto Pamphlet Award, Cúirt New Writing Prize and 2021 Gutter Edwin Morgan Prize.

My gratitude also to Damian Smyth and Arts Council NI for a 2019 Individual Artist award.

Thanks to all poets, reading groups and workshops who have helped me, in particular: Crescent Arts Centre, Community Arts Partnership, Poetry Ireland, The Stinging Fly, Arvon and Norwich Writers Centre; also to my fellow 'Hoors' from Poetry Ireland Introductions, poetry buddies forever. Moyra Donaldson, thanks for not throwing me out of your 2018 creative writing class, and for your valued mentoring and insight. To Helen Ivory, Stephen Sexton, Ruth Carr, Martina Evans, Fiona Sampson, Ann and Peter Sansom, Deirdre Cartmill, I am blessed to have your guidance and support. To my late teacher, who inspired me: Mr Sean Hollywood, formerly St. Colman's College, Newry, thank you.

To my parents, deepest gratitude for unending and unconditional love: thank you to my mother, Roseann, you are the gift that keeps on giving, and to my father, Bernard, in whose memory these poems are written.

Finally, to my family: for being my anchor and inspiration, my love forever.